Copyright © 2015
All rights reserved. This book or any portion thereof
may not be reproduced or used in any manner whatsoever
without the express written permission of the publisher
except for the use of brief quotations in a book review.

INTRODUCTION

It is my hope that this book takes you on that great voyage of self discovery that will help you uncover your hidden treasures.
Treasures that will become help you live the life you were meant to live and become the person you were born to be.
Make your mark in this world.
Leave something significant after you are gone.
Share your gifts with the others.
Be happy with your best efforts.
And remember everyone else is doing their best.

ABOUT THE AUTHOR

With 25 yrs of practice and teaching therapies designed to enhance human performance, Sean Connolly has developed a unique style of bringing the best out in everyone he meets

Motivational speaker, coach, author and TV personality Sean has delivered motivational talks to some of the UK's largest corporations and has been delivering his unique performance enhancement program to some of the worlds top athletes, dancers and musicians across the globe for the past 15yrs.

FORWARD

Welcome to self discovery!
This little book is packed with knowledge and questionnaires designed to weed out any doubt about your great abilities and to help water those seeds of self belief in your mind. Seeds that will grow into massive trees of personal power.

As with any journey, your journey of personal success and achievement must start with a destination in mind.
The vision of what you want and where you wish to be in the future.

Setting goals is a fundamental component to long-term success. The basic reason for this is that you can't get where you are trying to go until you clearly define where that is.
Research studies show a direct link between goals and enhanced performance in life. Goals help you focus and allocate your time and resources efficiently, and they can keep you motivated when you feel like giving up.

Just before we head off though on your journey , let us unload some of the extra baggage that you may be carrying that may hold you back.

Many people have been inspired to achieve a goal of some sort in the past only to be put off by others judging their performance or breaking down under stress and pressure due to a lack of self belief in being able to cope with challenges along the way.

So let us look at some of the obstacles that may hold you back from progressing towards your aspirations and goals in life.

THE FEAR OF THEM!

When you have a need for approval from other people around you, this means that you value the beliefs, opinions and needs of others above your own. Their opinion of you can become far more important to you than your own view of yourself. Receiving disapproval becomes a painful experience. Your entire decision making processes are eventually taken over by your need for the approval of others. You cannot take any decisive action without their approval. You sacrifice your own dreams and ambitions in order to have their approval.

Amongst the negative consequences of approval seeking behaviour are:

Lack of achievement

Lack of personal fulfilment .

Low self-esteem and confidence levels.

Reduced performance.

Increased stress.

You may argue that you do not engage in approval seeking behaviour. However, there are common behaviours which you may fail to recognise as approval seeking. Sometimes these behaviours are used as a tactical compromise, to keep the peace, or because the situation is not really that important to you. In some instances, as long as they are not too frequent, it may be useful to allow others to have their way. However, when these behaviours occur too frequently, or are motivated solely by a need for approval, you are adopting an unhealthy behaviour which can lead to severe problems.

Approval seeking behaviours:

The following are some of the most common approval seeking behaviours.

Changing or softening your position because someone appears to disapprove of your behaviour.

Feeling upset, worried, or insulted when someone disagrees with your opinion or suggestions.

Expressing agreement (verbally or non-verbally) when you do not agree with someone.

Doing something which you do not want to do because you are afraid to say 'No'

Spreading bad news and gossip to gain attention.

Consistently apologising for your words and deeds whether others have expressed disapproval or not e.g. 'I'm sorry but..'

Pretending to be knowledgeable or an authority on a subject because you are afraid to admit that there is something you do not know.

Attempting to coax people into paying you compliments and/or getting upset when they fail to do so.

Any behaviour which is contrary to your identity and purpose, or conflicts with your core beliefs, is generally done to gain the approval of someone else.

You are entitled to your own thoughts, beliefs and opinions. Just because you think differently to someone else it does not mean that one of you is right and one of you is wrong. It is important to be able to respect the right of others to have their own opinion but to do so; you must first be able to respect your right to have your own opinion. Respecting your own views requires you to avoid approval seeking behaviours.

The biggest irony with approval-seeking behaviour is that it usually produces the opposite results to those which are intended.

If you take a moment to consider those people whom you respect most, you will find that one of their strongest traits is their ability to be true to who they are. They will always stand up for what they believe in. Approval seeking behaviour is intended to get more approval and respect from others, yet what people generally respect is the very opposite i.e. people who are true to themselves. It is nice to have the approval of others but the way to get it is to have self-approval and self-respect. While modern life conditions people to seek approval; familiarising yourself with the approval seeking behaviours, listed above, will help you to identify when you are seeking approval, allowing you to take corrective action.

REDUCING ANXIETY AND STRESS

If the signs of anxiety at an important event are becoming too much for you it means that negative arousal has developed. Breathing will be faster, legs will feel heavy and shake and you may not be able to think straight . Sleep may also be difficult especially the night before the event.

You may not get enough hours , and if that is not bad enough, the hours you do get may not be as deep as desired either. In those cases the anxiety must be reduced. Many find that reading or listening to audios on visualisations work well.

Instead of thinking about what might happen, lie down and slowly relax your body and mind. The room may be darkened while the body is relaxed, starting from the extremities and slowly extending up to the centre of the body.

Your audios for relaxation, soft music or breathing exercises should be practiced or listened to during this time so that the ultimate result is lowered heart rate and breathing rates, resulting in better sleep.

Another treatment is massage. A long, slow full-body session will lower anxiety as well on an ongoing basis, perhaps weekly. These more frequent massages cut anxiety and release body toxins.

Thought Redirection

Another way to tame pre-performance jitters is to think of something else. Many young athletes, artists and entrepreneurs take little books such as this or my "The forgotten secret for success" book along to important events with them to replace negative thoughts with inspiring and motivational ideas about themselves.

Breathing exercises

Breathing exercises have been a part of many cultures promoting health and well being for centuries. When one is under stress they tend to breath very shallow and starve the body of vital oxygen.

An example of a simple but effective breathing exercise.
Take a slow breath in through the nose (for about 4 seconds)
 Hold your breath for 1 or 2 seconds.
Exhale slowly through the mouth (over about 4 seconds)
 Wait 2-3 seconds before taking another breath (5-7 seconds for teenagers)
Repeat for at least 5 to 10 breaths

Many times the feelings of anxiety we feel before a performance can remind us of previous times in our life when we experienced something that made us feel anxious afterwards.
This has the effect of fooling us into it happening again in the present moment or the future.
The best way to deal with this is to get rid of those bad memories and stop them repeating themselves over and over again.
Below is an example of such an exercise.

Exercise for removing bad memories

So is there a memory that keeps forcing itself into your mind's attention, and makes you feel bad?

Well, as you think about that memory now, with your eyes closed, notice that the image or movie of the memory in your mind has a location in space.

Is the image directly in front of you? Is it to the right? Or to the left?

Now attempt to move the picture towards you slightly then back into its usual position.

Have you noticed that you can reposition the picture?

Well now imagine in front of you a giant slingshot.

And notice the picture sitting in the centre of the slingshot if it is a movie place the TV in there.

Pull it back, and feel the tension in the elastic build in your mind and body as you stretch it all the way back, and let it go with a loud twang.

Now watch the picture shoot off until it's just a dot in the distance.

Think about something else for a moment such as what you ate last, then think of the memory again.

Is it in it's original position or has it moved?

Pull out your slingshot again and give it another go.

Keep doing this until the memory has no effect on your state at all and stays a dot in the distance when you think of it.

In my mind I keep a trash can and when I have a memory that is really annoying me I imagine it on a piece of paper, then reach out and scrunch it up, before dropping it into the trash can to my left with a satisfying crash.

Keeping a promise.

Have you ever had the experience of a friend or family member breaking a promise they made to you? Maybe you were promised that you would be taken somewhere special like a big game or a party and were let down at the last minute or forgotten about.

How does this make you feel when this happens? If people keep breaking promises to us we eventually begin to distrust them. This actually has the same effect when we break promises to ourselves. How many times have you made a promise to yourself that you would practice a specific skill that could enhance your performance in a chosen field? And then find an excuse that would prevent you from carrying out that extra practice.

Maybe you even made a promise to put in extra revision for academic work, or help your parents or a friend more. And then once again found an excuse to let yourself down.

If we keep breaking promise to ourselves that we have made, then we eventually come to the same conclusion as we came to with others who broke numerous promises. *That we cannot rely on ourselves!*

We should treat the promises that we make to ourselves just as importantly as those we have made to close friends. When we keep promises to ourselves we begin to trust ourselves.

Start your promises with some small tasks that will help you feel better about yourself and build self trust. Never make big promises that you feel will be hard to keep!

Some small examples are: I promise to read over and study my work 30 extra minutes each day. I promise to practice my new physical skills 30 minutes each morning and evening. I promise to look for opportunities to help my parents or a friend each day.

What small promises can you think of would help you become a better person?

I promise... I promise... I promise..

Never ever criticise yourself along your journey.
If you develop a habit of criticising yourself and suggesting that you are not a good person, there is the danger through time that you may actually believe it.
Many people in life never achieve anything in their life because they believe deep down they are not worth achieving or owning anything that will make them feel good.

1.Accept that you are a human, a member of the human race. We all make mistakes. This is why they put an eraser on top of a pencil!!

2. Realise that if you do not love and accept yourself, it will be almost impossible to accept love or friendship from anyone, as you won't believe that you deserve it.

3. Distance yourself from any critical thoughts that arise in your mind. Just step back and notice them while choosing to take action in the direction of things that you believe will make your life better.

4. Decide that you will appreciate yourself for your efforts and for what you have already achieved. Commit to staying focused on what is important to you and on what you wish to accomplish

5. Realise that self-criticism does not improve performance. It just makes you feel bad and may even hinder your making the changes you wish to make that will make you a better person.

6. Break down any large goals into manageable pieces. Focus on what the obstacles are and what it will take to overcome them.

7. Realise that success often involves failing first and learning from mistakes.

8. Decide to be the best you can be rather than comparing yourself to others.

9. Forgive yourself if necessary and move on

10. Focus on what you can control rather than the things you can't control.

Now we have got rid of some of that unwanted baggage and have fuelled up the vehicle, lets get back to the road map and decide where we want to go in the future.

Think about the "big picture." Ask yourself some important questions about what you want for your life?. The answers to this question can be as general as "I want to be happy knowing I always do my best" or "I want to help inspire younger people involved in my chosen field/sport to do well also. or "I want to be remembered as one of the great .... in years to come."

These general statements can help hone in on the things that really matter to you.

Recognising the things you value will guide your decision-making and keep you focused on your end goals.

Think of the answers to your "big picture" questions as things you hope to attain 10, 15, or 20 years from now

Break the "big picture" down into smaller and more specific goals.

Consider areas of your life that you either want to change or that you feel you would like to develop with time. Begin to ask yourself questions about what you'd like to achieve in each area of your life and how you would like to approach it within a one to five year timeframe. Look at your wheel of life an decide which area you need to work on and make stronger.

Use the SMART method to create actionable goals.

SMART is a mnemonic used by life coaches and motivators for a system of goal identification, setting, and achievement. Every letter in SMART stands for an adjective that describes an effective way to set goals.

•Specific. When setting goals, they should answer the highly specific questions of who, what, where, when, and why. Instead of the general goal, "I want to be a better ....," try for a specific goal, "I want to qualify for my first ....this year."

•Measurable. In order for us to track our progress, goals should be quantifiable. "I'm going to practice more" is far more difficult to track and measure than "Everyday I'm going to practice for an extra 30 minutes."

•Attainable. It is important to evaluate your situation honestly and recognise which goals are realistic, and which are a little far-fetched. Instead of, "I am going to win a world title this year" it might be more realistic to say, "I am going to break my personal best which can take me to another step towards the world championships."

•Relevant. Is this goal relevant to your life and to the "big picture" questions you have already asked yourself? Some good questions to ask yourself when figuring this out are: does it seem worthwhile? Is now the right time for this? Does this match my needs?

Time-related. Setting a "due date" to meet goals not only keeps you on track, but it prevents pesky daily roadblocks from getting in the way. Instead of saying "I'm going to get my college degree", you might consider saying, "I'm going to get my B.A. in 4 years."

Keep track of your progress.
Journaling is a great way to keep track of personal progress. Checking in with yourself and acknowledging the progress made towards a certain goal is key to staying motivated.
Asking a friend in class with similar goals to buddy-up with you is a great way to keep you motivated and to make sure you hit your goal target dates also.

Reward your accomplishments.
Acknowledge when you have reached goals and allow yourself to celebrate in your own way. Take this time to assess the goal process--from the start to completion.

•If you feel it took too long to achieve this goal, examine you stumbling blocks. Was your goal reasonable? Are there skills you may need to acquire before attempting to complete other goals? Do you feel worth it?

•If you learned something about the way you work towards meeting your goal, is it something that can be applied to other goals?

Are you confident that you can get there?

Positive questions to help you become a better person and understand yourself more.

Ask yourself the questions that give you the answers to progress. What's more, keep a written record of your answers to these questions. it's easy for them and be forgotten in time. If you have them written down, then you can review your notes and take it a step further, instead of answering the same questions all over again. Keep them in a notebook that's both easy to access and update wherever you happen to be; it will be a source of sustenance for you, by which you can continue to measure your growth through life.

So let's get you started.

"If I had all the resources in the world what would I be doing with my day to day life and why?"

Perhaps you'd be painting, or writing dance plays, or exploring different types of cultures. Don't hold back, just keep writing.

"What do I want to look back on in my life and say that I never regretted"?

  Would you regret never having traveled abroad?

Would you regret never having auditioned for a part in a show, a trial for a team or even a promotion even if it meant risking rejection?

Would you regret not spending enough time with your family when you could?

This question can be really difficult.

"If you had to choose three words to describe the kind of person you would love to be, what would those words be?"

Adventurous?

Loving?

Open?

Honest?

Hilarious?

Optimistic?

Don't be afraid to choose words that are considered negative because that proves you're a real person, and not a lopsided combination of parts other people want to be known for.

Sometimes the traits that you don't like become useful in dangerous situations (such as anger) for maybe dealing with a bully. Sometimes they are valuable to the job you're meant to perform correctly— like being fussy.

"Who am I?"

 This question is not static. It should be one you continue to ask yourself throughout your life. A healthy person continues to reinvent themselves throughout their life.

By asking this question regularly, it updates your understanding of who you are and how you change. Instead of answering who you think you ought to be, keep it focused on who you actually are.

GETTING THAT FEELING OF YES I CAN !

Like any feeling we experience as a human confidence will fluctuate in different circumstances in our life. This is why it is important that you keep reminders around you that will bring back this feeling when you need it. Reminders such as books, personal notes and audios.

Here is another exercise to keep cementing those building blocks of self esteem and confidence.

SELF CONFIDENCE WORKSHEET

Keep your completed self esteem worksheets handy. The next time you're feeling low self esteem and need a self esteem boost read your **Self Confidence** worksheet and be reminded of your personal power and use it to transform situations in which you feel less confident..

PART ONE

Think of a situations in which you experienced confidence and a feeling of satisfaction and self worth. Answer the following questions.

What where the situations?

What do you say to yourself about the situation (self talk)?

How do you feel physically? What sensations and feelings do you have in your body?

What did you do as a result of this?

What word, phrase, image or posture would remind you of this whole experience?

PART TWO

Think of a current situation in which you experienced a lack of confidence that you would like to change if you could.

What was the situation?

What do you say to yourself about the situation (self talk)

How do you feel physically?

What sensations and feelings do you have in your body?

What did you do as a result of this?

What word,phrase,image or posture would remind you of this whole experience?

PART THREE

Look at Part Two and using the information that you have learned about yourself in Part One, ask yourself - When I am in this situation:

1. What positive statement could I say to myself to be reminded of my power?

2. What could I do that would help me feel differently?

For example, create a visualisation, posture and phrase in which I remember how I felt in Part One.

3What could I do differently, next time I am in this situation?

4. What actions would empower me?

HOW TO AVOID THE FEELING OF "NO I CANT"

After taking the time to build self confidence, many people break it down again unintentionally.

Why do some people loose confidence after experiencing a loss or setback?

Highly committed people, including perfectionists, hurt their confidence with a harsh attitude about the way they have performed.

Top performers know they must learn from their mistakes and poor performances so they can improve, which leads to improved confidence instead of self-doubt.

They don't become discouraged or feel helpless when they fail to win or do not perform up to their expectations. They are able to regroup by assessing their strengths and weaknesses.

The strength of your mental game has everything to do with the level of your confidence. You want to do everything in your power to grow your confidence and be your own best friend.

3 Tips To Stay Confident After a Poor Performance.

1. Be more subjective about your performance - focus on a few things that went well and a few things you want to improve on.

2. Use mistakes as an opportunity to improve - make new goals and get motivation from what you've identified as to what you need to improve on.

Give yourself credit for what you did well during your performance - don't just focus on mistakes, acknowledge the parts that went well.

Making a self appreciation list

What makes you think you deserve all that you want to achieve in your life?

Is that a hard question to answer? Maybe you don't give yourself enough credit for all the things you are doing. Instead of thinking that you have to do all kinds of things in your daily life you might consider that you are a wonderful person that chooses to do them.

For it is a fact that nobody forces you to go to work, practice or study . You make that choice every single day for the benefit of yourself and others. Give yourself the credit of doing all those marvellous things each day that help you grow as a person and please your loved ones. Be proud of yourself in the same way that your parents and teachers where and are proud of you.

A great way of generating this feeling of appreciation for yourself is to make an appreciation list.

Make your Appreciation List by starting each sentence with 'I am so proud of myself for...'. Fill in every aspect of your life where you know you choose the right thing to do to contribute like 'I am so proud of myself for helping my Parents, friends, team or chosen charity.

'I am so proud of myself for writing this piece of work for school/ work/ group although I wanted to listen to music in stead. I am proud of myself for taking the time to cheer up a friend who was feeling sad. I am so proud of myself for working hard and getting the results my teacher/boss/coach knew I was capable of.

Go on and on until you feel a great sense of appreciation about yourself. Make sure you write or type the whole sentence starting with **'I am so proud of myself'** for it will focus your attention on the feelings of pride. If you have a hard time finding things to be proud of ask your parents/partner or a close friend to help you.

THE PLEASURE IS ALL MINE

The next time you are feeling unhappy take out your **Pleasure List** and do something on the list or imagine yourself doing something on the list. Then, notice your attitude change.

Shifting your focus, even for a moment, to something that you enjoy sends a clear message to your brain that says: "I deserve happiness." "I am in control of my thoughts and feelings." When you practice this activity you strengthen your self esteem muscle.

1. Make a List of the people and pets who bring a smile to your face when you think of them:

2. Make a List of the places that bring a smile to your face when you think of them:

3. Make a list of the things that bring a simile to your face when you think of them:

4. Make a list of the things you like to do that bring you pleasure:

Are you beginning to feel better about yourself, more confident, happy? Good! Let's keep building on this.

TOOT YOUR HORN WORKLIST

Complete the statements underneath. If you cannot answer an item, don't worry - simply complete what you can.

Keep your completed Self Esteem Worksheets handy. The next time you're feeling low self esteem and need a boost read your **Toot Your Horn** worksheet and reminded yourself of your natural resources and personal power.

1. I like myself because:

2. I'm an expert at:

3. I feel good about:

4.My friends would tell you I have a great:

5.My favourite activity is:

6.I'm loved by:

7.People say I am a good:

8.I've been told I have pretty:

9.I consider myself a good:

10.What I enjoy most is:

11.The people I admire the most are:

12.I have a natural talent for:

13.Goals for my future are:

14.I know I will reach my goals because I am:

15.People compliment me about:

16.I feel good when I:

17.I've been successful at:

18. I laugh when I think about:

19. The traits I admire myself for are:

20. I feel peaceful when:

KNOWING YOUR VALUES

Our values are those important rules that will live by and make decisions on, even when we are not aware of them. When you are aware of your own values you have gained a great source of self knowledge that can help you make decisions and give you direction in your life. You will also be aware of what activities you should avoid if they do not co exist with your values.

A list of life values.

Choose 10 that appeal to you the most, then prioritise your top five. Then number from 1 to 5 in order of importance to you.

These values should be a part of your ideal lifestyle and achievement statements for the future to make sure that you are living a life that matches your values.

For example, if your values where caring, success, helping, control and discovery, you could put these in a paragraph of how you would like to be in the future such as:

I want to be a great athletic coach in the future known for my caring, controlled style of teaching that will focus on skills as well as discovering new things about myself that will help my students develop in their life, and give me that feeling of success.

VALUE LIST.

Adventure Activities that are new and different for you.

Aesthetics Appreciating or study the beauty of ideas, surroundings or objects.

Attractiveness The appearance of yourself and others.

Belonging and Being accepted as a worthwhile member of a group.

Caring, Showing and compassion.

Helping those in need.

Career Achieving success in chosen field of work.

Challenging Problems Engaging in complex questions and demanding tasks.

Community Being part of a supportive community of people.

Competition and Participating in activities that pit personal skills and abilities against others.

Connectedness, Being close and connected to others.

Conformity, Acting and behaving within social norms.

Control Being in command of your environment and surroundings.

Cooperation Working and acting towards a common end or purpose.

Creative Expression Expressing your ideas in novel and unique ways. Having the opportunity for experimentation and innovation.

Discovery Exploring and identifying new approaches to the world.

Diversity Appreciating differences in people, ideas and situations.

Family Building and maintaining a close knit family.

Fairness Demonstrating a commitment to justice and the equal treatment of individuals.

Fidelity Being faithful and loyal to family and friends.

Health Maintaining a healthy body and mind.

Honesty Demonstrating truthfulness and sincerity.

Humility Demonstrating modesty in behaviour, attitude and spirit.

Independence Determining a course of action free from control by others.

Influence Being in a position to change attitudes or beliefs of other people.

Knowledge Engaging in the pursuit of scholarship, truth and understanding.

Leadership Having the ability to motivate and inspire others towards a common vision.

Loyalty Being steadfast in allegiance to people, ideals or customs.

Luxury Enjoying the richness of comforts and pleasures.

Nature Enjoyment of the outdoors. Honouring nature.

Passion Feelings of excitement and connection to people, purpose and activities.

Personal Growth Advancing and progressing in mind, body and spirit throughout life.

Pleasure Seeking satisfaction, sensual gratification and fun.

Pursuit of Excellence Performing tasks to the best of your ability.

Recognition Seeking positive feedback and acceptance for well done tasks.

Respect Recognising others' worth and right to self determination.

Responsibility Demonstrating ethical accountability for decisions and actions.

Risk taking Aspiring to the difficult, challenging and sometimes impossible.

Security Being free from fear, danger, or risk, to exist in a stable environment.

Self-Interest Having high regard for personal interests and advantages.

Sensitivity Being aware of and sensitive to the needs and wants of others.

Service Contributing to and being involved in efforts to help individuals or groups without motive or personal gain.

Simplicity Enjoying a simple non complex and excessive life. **Spirituality** Having awareness of the connection to a higher power, a world view that includes a higher purpose and meaning.

Status Gaining the respect of others.

Success Personal and professional lifelong achievement.

Tolerance Recognising and respect the opinions, practices and behaviours of others.

Trustworthiness Fulfilling commitments and keep promises.

Wealth Accumulating enough material possessions and money to free yourself from worry.

Variety Finding frequent change of activities and settings.

SEE IT, BELIEVE IT, ACHIEVE IT!!

Some Powerful reasons to use visualisation as part of your strategy to achieve your goals

Mental practice can get you closer to where you want to be in life, and it can prepare you for success! For instance, Natan Sharansky, a computer specialist who spent 9 years in prison in the USSR after being accused of spying for US has a lot of experience with mental practices. While in solitary confinement, he played himself in mental chess, saying: "I might as well use the opportunity to become the world champion!" Remarkably, in 1996, Sharansky beat world champion chess player Garry Kasparov!

A study looking at brain patterns in weightlifters found that the patterns activated when a weightlifter lifted hundreds of pounds were similarly activated when they only imagined lifting.

An exercise psychologist from Cleveland Clinic Foundation in Ohio, compared "people who went to the gym with people who carried out virtual workouts in their heads". He found that a 30% muscle increase in the group who went to the gym. However, the group of participants who conducted mental exercises of the weight training increased muscle strength by almost half as much (13.5%). This average remained for 3 months following the mental training.

Tiger Woods who has been using it since his pre-teen years. Seasoned athletes use vivid, highly detailed internal images and run-throughs of the entire performance, engaging all their senses in their mental rehearsal, and they combine their knowledge of the sports venue with mental rehearsal. World Champion Golfer, Jack Nicklaus has said: "I never hit a shot, not even in practice, without having a very sharp in-focus picture of it in my head".

Even heavyweight champion, Muhammad Ali, used different mental practices to enhance his performance in the ring such as: "affirmation; visualisation; mental rehearsal; self-confirmation; and perhaps the most powerful affirmation of personal worth ever uttered: "I am the greatest"".

Use all 5 Senses in Your Visualisation

1.Despite its name, visualisation should include more than just your eyesight. Imagine with all of your senses that what you dream is a reality. See the image in your minds eye, hear the sounds, taste it, smell it, and feel it in your body.

2. Get Dramatic and Act Out Your Visualisation

Be playful and use your imagination. Role-play is a great technique for kinaesthetic (Feeling) learners. Acting out your visualisation will help you feel in your body that your dreams are already a reality.

If it helps, have a partner act with you. For example, if you are trying to manifest a role in a professional show, have a partner pretend to be your lead dancer. The two of you can act out the show.

3. Use Props

Props are a great way to trick the unconscious mind into believing something is reality.

Actor Jim Carrey grew up in a poor family and would often dream of being an actor. He took his visualisations seriously and would imagine directors coming up to him and offering him acting jobs.

Jim is famous for using props in his visualisations. He once wrote himself a check for 10 million dollars, dated it a few years in advance, and wrote, "for acting services rendered" in the memo line. Just a few months before the check date, he received 10 million dollars for his role in Dumb & Dumber.

Be creative when using props. But, make them seem as realistic as possible. For example, if you are trying to manifest getting a role in a show or winning a Olympic medal, practice receiving the medal or wear similar costumes to those performers in the show when practicing at home.

4. Meditate Immediately Prior to Visualisation

Meditation will put you in a relaxed open state, which allows your visualisation to penetrate you on a deeper level. Relaxing the mind will help silence your mind and clear out any negative thoughts, beliefs, fears, and doubts that will hold you back from achieving your goals.

5. Visualise Several Times a Day

The more you visualise, the better. Use moments of down time to practice short 2-3 minute visualisations.

6. Write Your Visualisations Down

Write your visualisations down using descriptive language. The memory system responds well to the written word and this will reinforce the ideas in your mind, particularly if you have a visual learning style.

7. Create a Vision Board

A vision board will make your visualisation tangible. Use photographs, magazine cutouts, and other items to create a vision board of your goal. Look at it frequently to remind you of that which you hope to accomplish.

8. Be Within Your Own Limits

For best results, start out visualising that which is believable to you. Once you start seeing results, then you may find that you are able to stretch your limits even further after seeing the true creative power you hold in your life.

9. Be Proactive

Jim Carrey once stated on the Oprah Show, "Visualisation works if you work hard. That's the thing.

—

Visualisation is not magic. You still have to put in effort when trying to <u>achieve a goal</u>.

I hope that you find these visualisation strategies effective at manifesting what you want in your life. Each of us possesses a unique and creative source of infinite potential within us. Unlock yours by retraining your brain and releasing your limiting beliefs, fears, and doubts that hold you back.

Unlock your mind

Harry Houdini the legendary magician illusionist and escape artist was famous for escaping from prisons, submerged trunks, bank vaults, and jumping off bridges into rivers covered in ice.

For example, in one of his most famous and spectacular feats, he broke out of Scotland Yard, even though one of the conditions of the challenge was that he be allowed NO clothing whatsoever — in order to keep him from concealing tools or keys.

So how did he do it?

Quite simple, really. Using a razor blade, he cut a small, invisible slit in a heavy callous on his heel. Under this tiny flap of hardened skin, he concealed a small piece of watch spring. Then, once he was alone, he used this little strip of metal to pick all the locks. He then tossed the tool away and walked out!

Looking to capitalise on Houdini's immense popularity and fame, a London bank challenged him to break out of their vault with its new, state-of-the-art locking system. They were CERTAIN that even the great Houdini would finally meet his match.

Houdini accepted, and on the appointed date, the press turned out in droves to see if the master could get out in the three and a half minutes allotted.

This time he got to keep his clothes on. But he had another trick up his sleeve!

His contracts always specified that before he disappeared into the trunk or cell or behind a small curtain (when performing on a stage), he could kiss his wife. After all, many of his feats were seriously dangerous, so who could refuse the couple what might turn out to be their last goodbye?

But what no one knew was that he was getting more than a kiss! As their lips met, his wife would secretly pass a small piece of wire from her mouth to his. Then, once he was alone or hidden behind the curtain, he'd use the wire to pick the locks.

This time out, though, the wire didn't seem to be doing the trick. Here's what Houdini wrote about that experience ...

"After one solid minute, I didn't hear any of the familiar clicking sounds. I thought, my gosh, this could ruin my career, I'm at the pinnacle of fame, and the press is all here.

"After two minutes, I was beginning to sweat profusely because I was not getting this lock picked.

"After three minutes of failure, with thirty seconds left, I inadvertently reached into my pocket to get a handkerchief and dry my hands and forehead, and when I did, I leaned against the vault door and it creaked open."

And there you have it, my friend. The door was never locked! But because Harry BELIEVED it to be locked, it might as well have been. Only the "accident" of leaning on the door changed that belief and saved his career.

It's the same way with all of us. The things we believe to be insurmountable barriers, obstacles, and problems are just like the bank vault door. The only lock is in our minds, and as long as we simply believe that we CAN'T, well, we can't.

But when we give the door a push we can be amazed to find that not only is the door not locked to us, there's really no door at all, just the illusion of one.

We can all be master magicians. All we have to do is face whatever barrier seems to be looming before us, then take the first step, give the door a shove. The biggest obstacles are the ones we have created ourselves in our minds, and when we give our focus, faith, and feeling to them, THEY become our vision — and then they become real.

Good luck and enjoy your journey!!

Make sure to go over your notes once a week as consistency is a vital ingredient in the formula for success.

I sincerely hope you continue to move towards your true goals of health, happiness and contentment in your life.

Best regards.

Sean Connolly.

www.seanconnolly.info

#Dancingminds

instagram : Dancingminds

www.ingramcontent.com/pod-product-compliance
Lightning Source LLC
Chambersburg PA
CBHW050805240726
48654CB00008B/638